Needle Felting Gnome Simplified For Beginner's With Ease

The Complete Easy To Follow Step By Step Picture Guide On How To Needle Felt Gnome And Any Other Felting Craft Projects

Petrina Purser

TABLE OF CONTENTS

INTRODUCTION

In the realm of creating, needle felting is probably the cutest action around. It's basic in idea yet glances complex in execution, and the outcomes are intricate models made totally out of fleece. Basically, the movement utilizes an extraordinary needle to meld strands in a hardened structure. Creatures are a famous subject for needle felting as their genuine fluffiness is ideal for the fluffiness of the filaments.

Needle felting is a technique for felting without the utilization of water, which is utilized in most other felting applications. The strategy utilizes a pointed or indented needle to tangle the individual filaments together to frame pictures and shapes. The main needle felting supplies are simply the needles, felting needles can be utilized each in turn or in a gathering using a handle/holder. Single needles are utilized for subtleties while gatherings of needles make more extensive base shapes.

CHAPTER 1

MATERIALS AND TOOLS YOU NEED

Wandering for the body

Wandering for the head and nose

Meandering for the cap

Meandering for the facial hair

Felting cushion (piece of froth, wipe, pad you couldn't care less about, pocket loaded up with rice. Simply something you can put your piece on and cut into)

Fine felting needle (40 measure is my inclination)

CHAPTER 2

FORMING THE BODY

Get some wandering of the shading you need the body to be.

Fold it over your multiple times. Recollect that in the wake of felting the body will be more modest and more limited than it is around your finger.

Take it off your finger and spot it on your felting mat.

Jab at it while turning it. At this stage we're not genuinely attempting to shape it, simply get all the fleece got so it doesn't effectively fall apart or unroll. When you can take your piece off the matt and not have any free pieces standing out, you're prepared to move to the following stage.

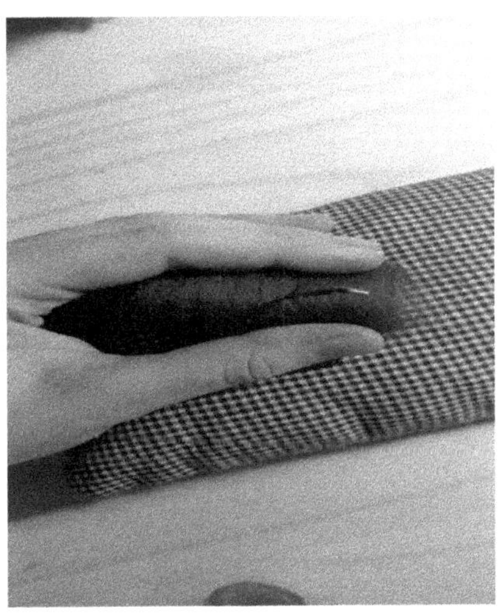

To felt the base and the top, snatch a portion of the meandering with your needle and jab it down on the opposite side. Basically, you need to crease a tad of each side over to guarantee you get a pleasant base.

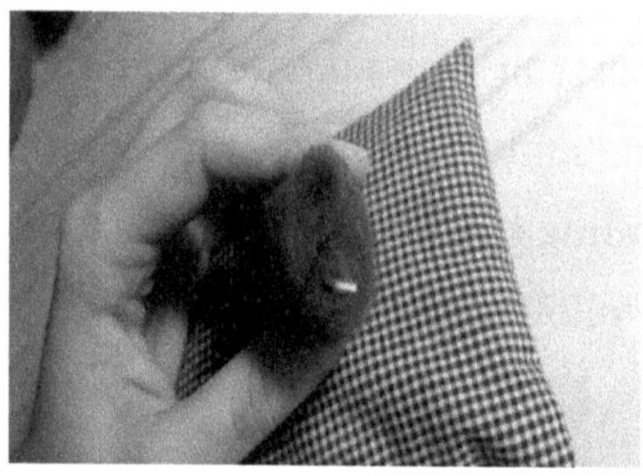

Continue to jab at it till you get the shape and immovability you need. Keep in mind, you can hold the meandering in the shape you need it to be with one hand and wound with the other.

CHAPTER 3

FORMING THE HEAD

Get a portion of your skin hued wandering. It'll be somewhat short of what you utilized for the body.

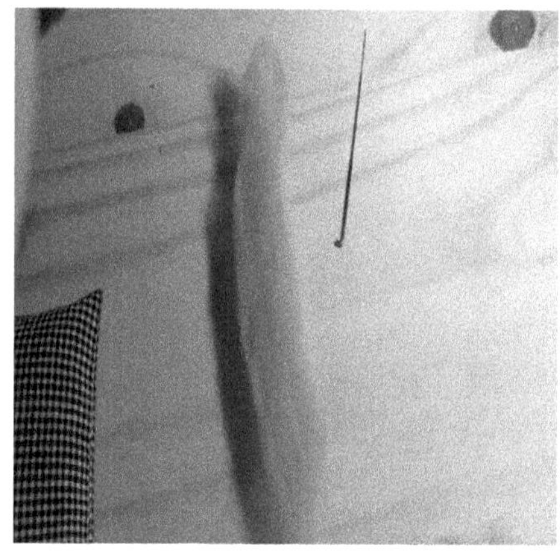

Once more, fold it over your finger to generally frame the shape.

Take it off your finger and jab at it while turning it around on the felting cushion.

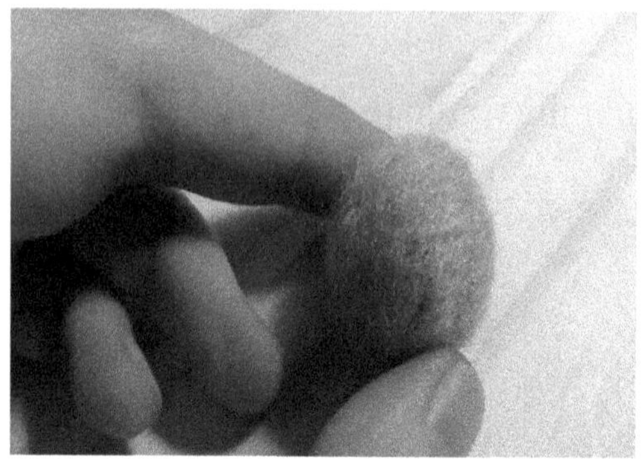

Continue to cut till it's the shape and size you need.

CHAPTER 4

FORMING THE HAT

Same thing once more, get some meandering the shading you need the cap to be, it'll be a comparative add up to what you utilized for the body.

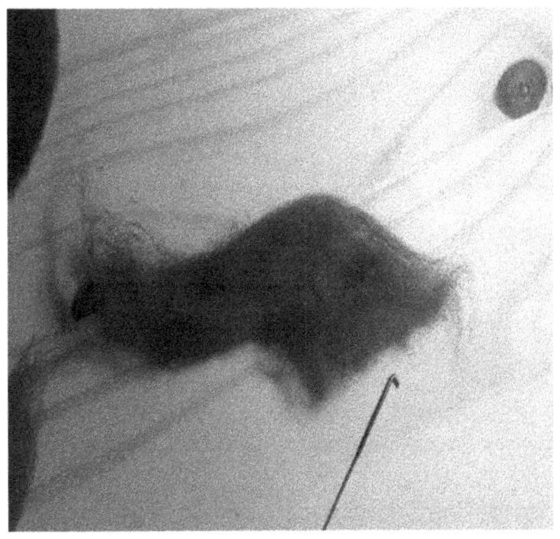

Fold it over your finger and afterward jab at it on the mat with the goal that it doesn't unroll.

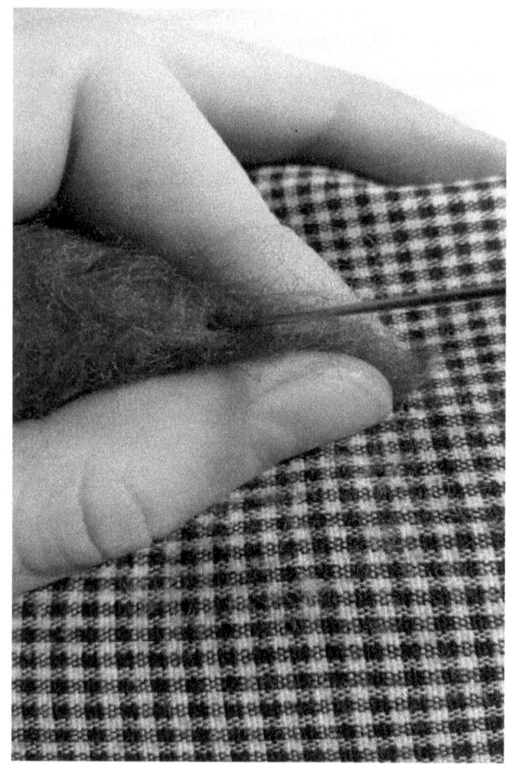

Squeeze one finish of it between your fingers to shape a point. While standing firm on it in that footing jab the wandering to keep it in that shape.

Wound away till it's the shape and size you need!

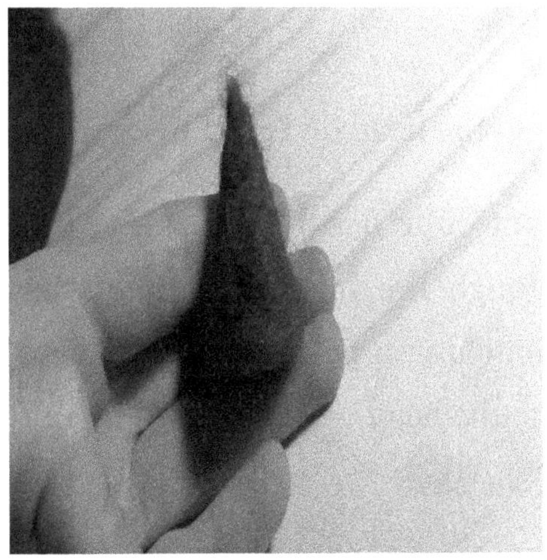

CHAPTER 5

INTERFACING THE HEAD TO THE BODY

Hold the head on top of the body.

Point your needle slantingly so it goes through the highest point of the body (snatching a portion of that fleece) and into the head.

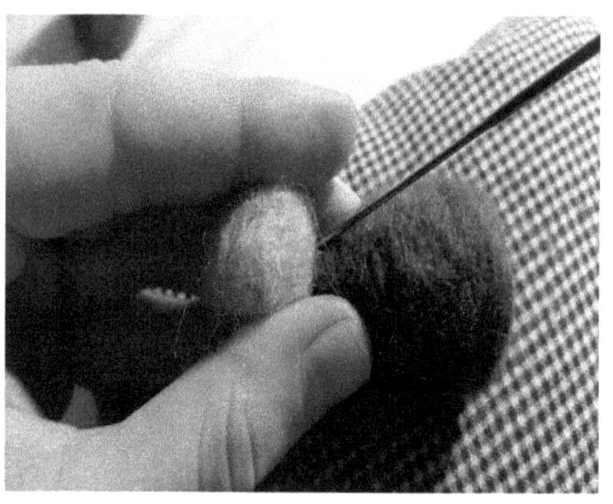

Circumvent the head felting like that to assist with getting the head.

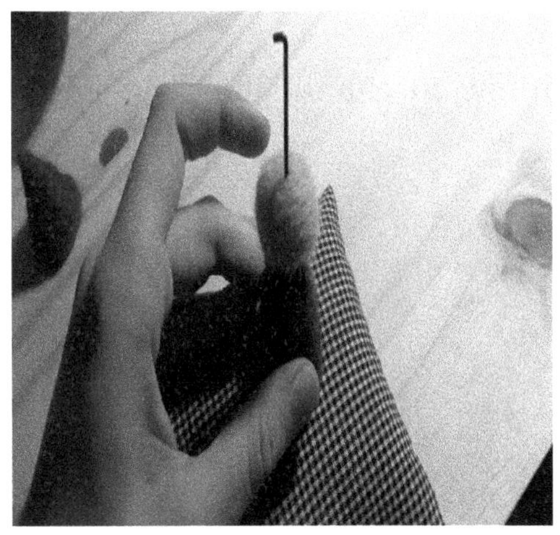

Presently go from the highest point of the head straight down to the body. You don't have to bring your needle right back out since we're making an effort not to shape the head, simply tangle the head strands with the body ones. At the point when you do this, consider where the spikes are on your needle and ensure they are diving adequately deep to go into the body.

Continue to cut till the head is safely joined!

CHAPTER 6

CONNECTING THE HAT TO THE HEAD

Position the cap where you'd like it to be on the body.

Searched the edge of the cap to append it.

CHAPTER 7

CONNECTING THE NOSE

Get a limited quantity of the skin shaded meandering.

Roll it between your palms to generally frame it into a ball.

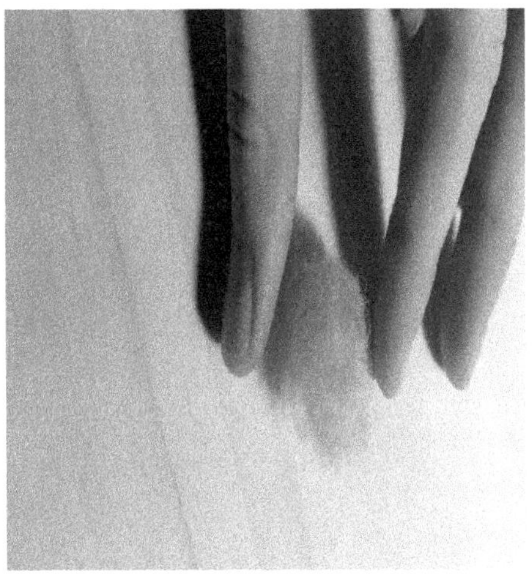

Cut it into a ball!

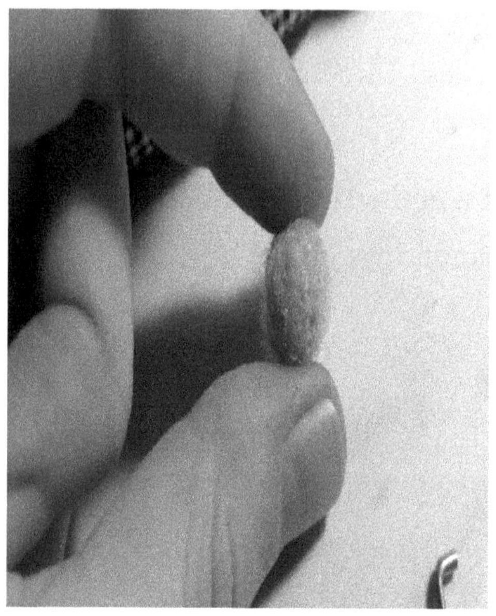

Wound it onto the head!

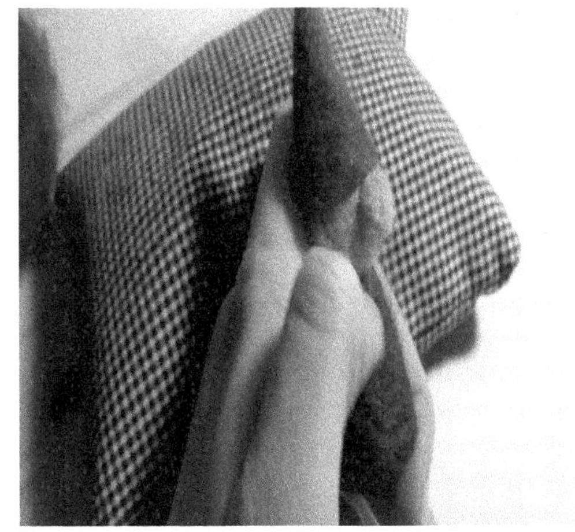

CHAPTER 8

FORMING THE HAIR AT THE BACK OF THE HEAD

On the off chance that you have a touch of room behind the cap where the head is appearing, we're going to cover it with some hair hued fleece.

Get a little wisp of the hair hued meandering.

Lay it along the rear of the head between the cap and the body.

Felt it into place.

Try not to stress a lot over how you felt down the pieces around the front of the face. Those will be concealed in the subsequent stage.

CHAPTER 9

FORMING THE IMPORTANT FACE BEARDS

Facial hair time!

Snatch a wisp of the facial hair growth hued meandering.

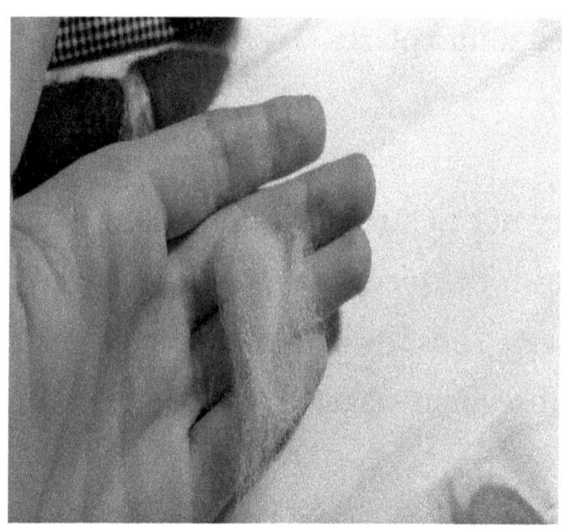

Overlap it fifty-fifty with the goal that it resembles the image above.

Felt the up part and under the nose along the face.

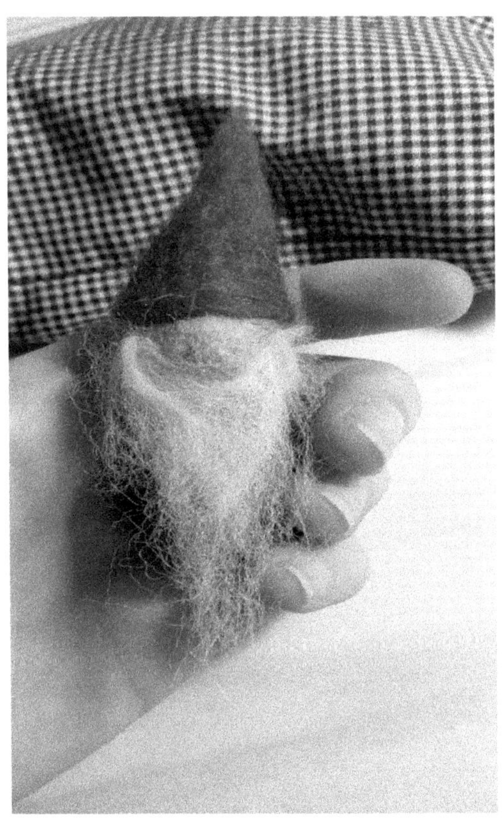

Rehash to add on another layer or two.

Felt the facial hair down into place. I like to give it a little twist toward the end, yet that is dependent upon you!

CHAPTER 10

ULTIMATE RESULT

THE END

Milton Keynes UK
Ingram Content Group UK Ltd.
UKHW020812050124
435493UK00013B/1797